Active Volcanoes

W9-BDK-709

Contents

Introduction 2

How an Active Volcano Erupts 4

What Comes out of Active Volcanoes 6

Types of Volcanic Eruptions 14

Glossary 23

Index 24

Written by Rose Goldsmith

Introduction

There are many volcanoes around the world.
Some of these volcanoes will not erupt again.
Volcanoes that will not erupt again
are called extinct volcanoes.

Some volcanoes have not erupted
for many years, but they could erupt again.
Volcanoes that could erupt again
are called dormant volcanoes.

Some volcanoes are still erupting.
These volcanoes are called active volcanoes.

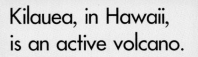

Kilauea, in Hawaii,
is an active volcano.

How an Active Volcano Erupts

The outer part of Earth is called its **crust**.
There are openings, called **vents**, in the crust.
It is very hot under the crust.
It is so hot that parts of the rocky crust melt.
The red-hot melted rock is called **magma**.

The surrounding solid rock
presses down on the magma,
forcing it to escape upward, toward the crust.
A volcanic eruption happens
when the magma comes out, or erupts,
through a vent.

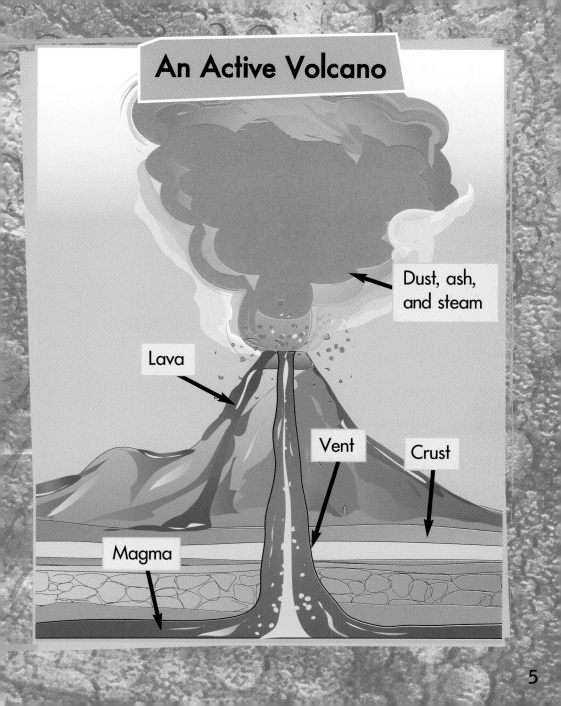

An Active Volcano

Dust, ash, and steam

Lava

Vent

Crust

Magma

5

What Comes out of Active Volcanoes

When the magma comes out of a vent
in Earth's crust, it is called **lava**.
Lava is very hot.
It can be runny like warm honey
or it can be pasty like soft clay.

Red-hot lava is thrown out of a volcano.

Lava is not the only thing
that comes out of volcanoes.
Sometimes, pieces of red-hot rock
blow out of the top
of a volcano with the lava.

This scientist is studying a chunk of lava from Kilauea volcano.

Dust often comes out of Earth
when a volcano erupts.
A strong volcanic eruption can throw the dust
as far as 18 miles away from the volcano.
Sometimes, the dust gets blown
around the world.

Ash often comes out of Earth
in a volcanic eruption.
If the hot ash falls into rivers,
it can mix with the water and form boiling mud.
A boiling mud river can be very dangerous.

Dust and ash blowing out of Soufriere Hills volcano in Montserrat, West Indies

Gas and steam also come out of Earth
in most eruptions.
Most of the steam
comes from a volcano's magma,
but it can also come
from hot water in the ground.
There is often dust mixed with the steam,
which makes it look like black smoke.

Clouds of smoke-like gas and steam erupting from Mount St. Helens in the United States of America.

Types of Volcanic Eruptions

You may think that all volcanic eruptions
are the same, but they are not.
Some eruptions are so strong
that they can blow mountains apart.
Others are so weak
that you can stand close enough
to watch the lava flow out.

This scientist is walking along a slope close to a lava flow.

Mauna Loa in Hawaii is a volcano
that has been formed by weak eruptions.
The lava does not blast from the vent,
it just spills out and runs over the ground.
When the lava cools, it becomes hard.
When the volcano erupts again, more hot lava
flows on top of the cold, hard lava.
Then the hot lava cools
and becomes hard.

With each eruption, more lava flows,
cools, and becomes hard.
The hard lava builds up each time,
until it forms a mountain.

Lava flowing from Hawaii's Mauna Loa, the largest volcanic mountain on Earth

Paricutin, in western Mexico,
is another mountain that was formed
by a weak eruption.
This volcano started in a cornfield
when hot ash came out of a vent.
The hot ash cooled and became hard.

Each time the volcano erupted,
more hot ash cooled and became hard.
Paricutin erupted for nine years.
By then, the vent in the cornfield
had turned into a mountain.

Paricutin volcano in Mexico,
blowing out ash clouds

In 1815, Mount Tambora erupted in Indonesia.
The mountain was about 13,100 feet high.
It lost much of its top
in the strong eruption.

Nearly 70 years later, also in Indonesia,
there was another strong volcanic eruption.
The volcano that erupted was Krakatau.
This eruption was so loud that people as far as
3,000 miles away heard the blast.

Krakatau volcano stands about 2,600 feet above sea level.

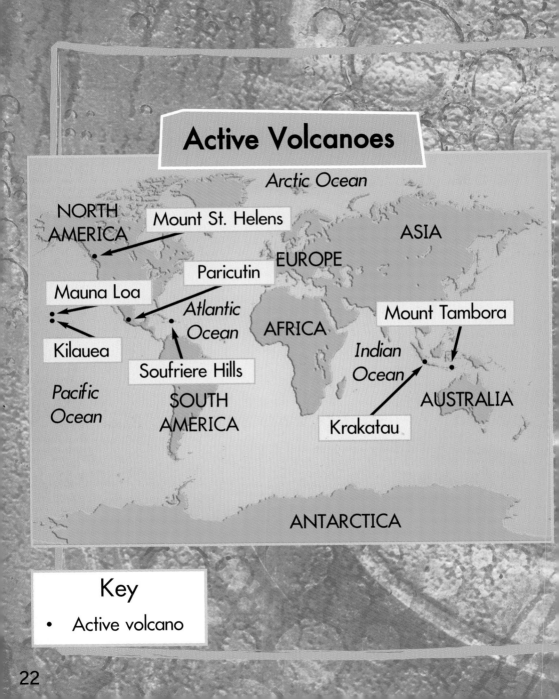

Active Volcanoes

Arctic Ocean

NORTH AMERICA

Mount St. Helens

ASIA

EUROPE

Paricutin

Mauna Loa

Atlantic Ocean

AFRICA

Mount Tambora

Kilauea

Soufriere Hills

Indian Ocean

Pacific Ocean

SOUTH AMERICA

AUSTRALIA

Krakatau

ANTARCTICA

Key

• Active volcano

Glossary

ash...the powder that is left after something has been burned

crust...the rocky outer layer of Earth

lava...hot liquid rock that flows out of a volcano

magma...melted rock beneath Earth's crust

vents...openings in Earth's crust

Index

crust 4–6

eruption(s). 4, 10, 12, 14, 16, 18, 20

lava. 5–9, 14–17

magma 4–6, 12

vent(s). 4–6, 16, 18